Blood and Water

ọbara na mmiri

Catherine Okoronkwo

First published in 2020
by Waterloo Press (Hove)
95 Wick Hall
Furze Hill
Hove BN3 1NG
Printed in Palatino 10pt by
One Digital
54 Hollingdean Road
East Sussex BN2 4AA

Cover image: © by Sumanjit K Johal

Author photograph © Catherine Okoronkwo 2020

A CIP record for this book is available from the British Library

ISBN: 978-1-906742-89-8

Acknowledgments

Thank you to everyone who has supported, encouraged, and believed in me on my journey as a writer. Many thanks to all my MA writing tutors at Manchester Metropolitan University who taught me much about crafting poems. Thank you to the editors of the University of Chester anthology *Crossings Over* (2017), in which the poem 'Change' was first published. Thank you to Chris Fewings who has mentored and supported me along the way. A massive thank you to Sumanjit K Johal who designed the stunning front cover image. Thank you to Waterloo Press, Akila Richards, John O'Donoghue, Naomi Foyle and Dan Locke, for their input in developing this work to publishable standard. And, finally, a huge thank you to my family and God who have given me the strength and courage to live, to breathe, and to write.

Dedication:

for my mother and father,
my sister and brothers,
my daughter

Contents

Instead, one of the soldiers pierced his side with a spear, and at once blood and water came out.

John 19:34 NRSV

This is the one who came by water and blood, Jesus Christ, not with the water only but with the water and the blood. And the Spirit is the one that testifies, for the Spirit is the truth.

1 John 5:6 NRSV

I am rooted, but I flow.

Virginia Woolf

Blood

ọbara

Mama Ukwu
Grandmother

She sleeps and her lower lip droops
toward age-sagged chest. Saliva drips
off the corner of her mouth; drops
elongate, fall on her print wrapper.
She looks like a Dodo.

Despite her diminutive stature, Grandmother
is fierce. Her expression, rarely warm,
crumpled; screwed up, as if permanently
dissatisfied with the smell of something
or the sight of someone.

My mother and grandmother disagree
on everything. Once: Grandmother
accused her of trying to poison
my father. Eyeing my mother's *okazi* soup,
my father refused his wife's pot for a month.

My mother prayed her husband would stay.
Grandmother, doubly bent over, was full
of smiles that day, as she swept the yard.
Unusual for her – as if some deity
were tickling her ribs with a taro leaf.

She died years later. Bronchitis
defeated her in the end. Just as she
did in sleep, she looked like a Dodo
in death. I wasn't troubled when she died,
didn't miss her suffocating curses.

She hated my mother and I hated her.

Papa Ukwu
Grandfather

On a carved stool,
he gulps Ovaltine,
fans firewood in the yard.

In a cast-iron pot,
plucked chicken,
feathers on the ground.

He rises in sandalled
feet, mutters incantations
to a host of silent gods.

From *anwụrụ* box,
scoops tobacco in nostrils.
Chews kola nut.

Eyes closed, hand raised,
begs with a guttural voice:
'May *ágbàrà* accept our gift.'

The Feast

Tongue lolls, blood gushes,
rushes onto baked Omoba soil.

My witchdoctor grandfather
carves up the carcass; spends hours

cleaning, praying and splaying.
The stink tickles the air.

Seven-year-old eyes transfixed
by the smirk on the dead creature's jowls.

The goat with a slit throat –
has he breathed his last bleat

or *mmuo mmiri* thrown him a lifeline?

mmuo mmiri – water spirit

[7]

Dead and Dying

A charred foetus
abandoned on Aba-Owerri
road. A youth under a torn
umbrella mends shoes.
Ashes and sparks scatter
in the harmattan wind.

A woman balances a basket
of coconuts to sell. Sweat
blisters on bleached skin.
A wild silhouette falls,
hand flails through a tyre,
in orangey-red flame.

Stomachs of young and old
gather round a wide-eyed cow.
The air, dry and clogged
with burning rubber, masks
the stench of gutters, rotting waste,
the dead and dying.

Only a Boy Counts

'I don't have any children,'
drunk Uncle Otti declared.
His teenage girls and I sat
huddled on the living room floor.

He wagged, swaggered, burped,
dazed by the effect of palm wine,
and repeated: 'God has cursed
my first wife. I have no heir.'

Years later, he took a younger
bride. Sixteen, uneducated, silent.
Redeemed by wide hips able
to conceive a plump baby boy,

she took charge of the main house,
shooed away my uncle's prettier
first wife. These events highlighted
my mother's many insecurities,

fears birthed out of miscarriages,
producing two female seeds. After
two decades of prayer-fuelled fights,
she delivered that desired boy-child.

Pumpkin Moon

'Am I following it?'

Pumpkin lodged in Omoba sky.
My young fanny tampered
by Uncle Innocent's paws.

On frayed mat, nicotine-tinged room,
I wriggle, bewildered —
my movements spellbound.

I imagine, the magic of strange
coloured glow. Pumpkin moon
reaches into my soul, transports

me from life's gaudy gloom.

Uncle Okoro

Behind the water tank, Nneka
and I spy on a lone lank figure.
'Who on earth is that?' She points.
'It's my Uncle Okoro,' I murmur.
'He looks like a falcon,' she says.

He sits on the verandah wall,
taps tobacco tin, scoops a finger-
load of powder, and stuffs nostrils.
Left, right. Taps again. Right, left.
He pinches his nose, and spits.

He doesn't budge for a long while,
then mutters and shakes his head.
As if reliving yesterday's events.
His daughter passed to the other side,
took her three weeks to be dead.

All hush-hush when she arrived,
the nature of her illness not to be spoken of.
Uncle Okoro carried her to the room.
What a waste, the relatives preened
for many days after they heard.

'My knees are hurting,' Nneka says,
as an iguana scuttles over our legs.

Bananas and Groundnut

I'll race you to Port-Harcourt,
we'll feast on bananas and groundnut...

I whispered this to my boyish uncle.
His wrist chained to a metal pole
wedged, in the middle of the compound.

Beneath Umugbede skies he writhed,
squat, or sat, legs outstretched.
Chained up all day and all night –

that's where he cussed, ate and pissed.
His malodour, rotten cassava, clings
to the dust. A fire burns in the distance.

In-between People

A story my mother told me.

One late night, amid busking katydids,
she journeyed from Omoba to Aba town.
The emergency? A dying distant relative.

Travelling over a low bridge, lying over
shallow water, she saw 'them'. Young
and old: splashing, washing, bathing, laughing . . .

The in-between people, their inky silhouettes.
'Don't make a sound,' her mother said,
'The living should never intrude on the dead.'

Calabash Bowl

overflows with water from the lake
will my neck snap under its weight?

Ike Seeks Asylum

He walked through a singed field
of broken bodies: machete slashes,
bullet wounds, bulged stomachs.

The clay and mud brick chapel
held their silent laments; vultures
hissed and circled red skies.

He remembered Aunty Ngozi,
gang-raped by youths who were
starved, angry and sullied.

She lay beside a pineapple clump,
her braided hair matted with blood
and semen, vomit and Guinness.

He drank *gari* and water for a week,
cursed Chukwu, demanded 'why?'
and abandoned the land of his forefathers.

Prayer Man

No older than eleven, piled in the back
seat with my parents, jolting down long
dirt roads to a hut at the forest's edge.

My mother insists on taking me
to prayer men who claim to keep
lives on an unfettered course. Today,
the Prayer Man will cast out the demon

threatening my future. Mother doesn't want
my chances of a wealthy husband or
a healthy child ruined by a curse.

The Prayer Man lights numerous candles
around my upright figure, starts shouting,
as if his god uses a hearing aid. I am faint
with the perfume of scented wax. I turn

to see my mother on a bench. My father
waits outside. Mother with a look:
Squeeze your eyes shut. The chants

get louder and more frightening, a flow
of words I can't decipher. He moves me
in anti-clockwise rotations, pauses,
rubs knuckles against my temple, screams

'It's coming. It's coming. It's coming.'
He holds out cupped palms, reveals
broken glass and nails of all sizes:

'From your head. The curse is dead.'
In the car, my stomach cramps
as if voodoo has found a new home,
now lodged in the pit of my belly.

Omoba Village 1982

One evening, I witness my Uncle Okoro carrying our cousin, Ugochi, from the front gates to the backyard. The fear and disgust in my mother's expression are palpable. Without another word, she turns and goes back into our house to the kitchen where she is preparing periwinkle soup. My eyes are transfixed by the deliberate movement of Uncle Okoro. I can't believe the bundle in his arms is Ugochi.

Two years before, Ugochi, a slender girl with shapely hips, brimmed with boundless laughter. An African gazelle, full of youthful exuberance, she had returned to Omoba village for a visit after many months away. When she came home, she arrived on an *okada* dressed in a yellow cotton gown, carrying a small worn suitcase. There had been a feast of pepper soup and jollof rice to welcome back this prodigal daughter. Searching for a life beyond the poverty of her parents and kin, Ugochi had travelled to Lagos, lined her pockets with the excesses of businessmen, and set up a hairdressing stall. That summer, she braided my hair, talking all the while about her life in the big city: the fish sellers, the traffic, the hum of generators, the satellite dishes hanging off buildings, the mechanics and market traders, and the opulence of hotels where Lebanese and Russians splash their cash on a girl who sways and sashays in the right way. I didn't know what she meant, but I was captivated by her stories. It didn't seem to matter that she hadn't finished secondary school – she was on her way up and out of the slow death of village life. She no longer had to fan wood for an open fire, fetch water from the local stream, or spend hours on the farm. She always said, 'Village life is no life.'

But now, in Uncle Okoro's arms, I see her skeletal contours beneath the tie-dye wrapper Uncle Okoro uses to hide her. She is barely moving.

She dies three days later.

*

Some years after, another cousin, Nneka, dies suddenly. She lived in Port Harcourt with her sister, Aunty Rose, and Uncle Tenta, a wealthy businessman. Rose is fair skinned, delicate and stunning. Her only flaw? She cannot have children. Uncle Tenta – black, stout and brutish, resembles a bulldog – beds any young girl within his reach. Despite Aunty Rose's prayers, eventually, Uncle Tenta takes to sleeping with his wife's sister, Nneka. With his oil money, he funds Nneka's Management course at the university.

One weekend, Aunty Rose sends Nneka to us in Omoba village. They want my grandfather, the witchdoctor, to terminate the life growing inside her. Together, Nneka and I walk out of the main house from the front. Our feet heavy on gravelled ground, we walk past lofty spiked gates, the expansive ube tree, travel round the right-angled bend, alongside a stretch of thick and overgrown shrubbery, turn right and enter the yard at the back. Through the windows of the kitchen in the main house overlooking the yard, I hear my mother clatter pots and pans over the stove. The small house which is home to my paternal grandparents is on the left. From behind a door, Papa Ukwu tells us to wait. We sit on the verandah wall. Nneka is wearing a fitted black skirt and a patterned blouse, as if dressed for an interview. Small in stature, beads of sweat on her forehead, her face is tight with worry. I stare at the red sandals on her feet, reminded of the summer of Ugochi's death, in that storeroom. I had not been in it since.

The swishing of a traditional broom pricks my ears; Mama Ukwu sweeping her room. All around crickets echo. Papa Ukwu appears with a lantern, a largish leather bag, and his stool. He hands the stool to me and makes his way to the middle of the yard. More crunch and gravel. He collects the stool and places it down. Palm, bamboo and plantain trees encircle the compound, casting shadows around us. Papa Ukwu sits down, coughs, asks me to go to the living room to retrieve his snuff box. When I return, Papa Ukwu is upright, eyes closed. Around his bare feet: the lantern, an egg, a feather, stones of differing shapes and sizes, a lizard's tail, and a coconut. The emptied leather bag lies like a sleeping dog beside the stool. I move closer.

[18]

Papa Ukwu doesn't seem to notice us, absorbed in a chant. He mutters in Igbo – words flow and fall into each other. I don't understand what he is saying. His gestures – arms outstretched ahead, then heavenwards – are fluid; make him taller, even youthful. This carries on for many minutes when without warning he opens his eyes and asks for his snuff box. I hand it over. He taps it twice with his index finger, scoops a heap of black and takes it to his teeth. He rubs the powder over browned enamel and coats the insides of his cheeks. Taking another heaped scoop, he sniffs it – a nostril at a time. His narrow shoulders heave with the pleasure of each intake. When our gaze meets again, he smiles and says, 'It's time to talk to the gods'. He falls to his knees and bows his head. No words are uttered, but his mouth is moving. After what seems an age, he lights the lantern, cracks the coconut and pours the egg into it. He places the lizard's tail inside and uses the feather to stroke the shell of the coconut, before placing the coconut on the ground, surrounding it with the stones. More prayers are said over the concoction before he commands Nneka to drink it. She does, without flinching. This was the last time I saw Nneka alive.

*

I am on holiday in Jerusalem when my mother tells me Nneka died. When I ask her 'Of what?' she hesitates, purses her mouth and says, 'Is it not the same thing that Ugochi died of?' It's not a question, rather a statement. I press her, because I want to know, what they died from. Another stretch of silence. Finally she says, in a barely audible voice, 'AIDS. That's what killed them.'

Finally, I knew the name of the illness that was not to be spoken about. Both my cousins had died of an AIDS-defining illness. According to WHO (2018), nearly 1 in every 25 adults on the African continent live with HIV. This was the sickness that could not be named because of the stigma and shame it carried. The vision of my uncle carrying that half-conscious figure of Ugochi sloping into the secret and stained world of those living with HIV and AIDS has

[19]

always stayed with me. The memory of Nneka gulping a coconut concoction my Papa Ukwu had prepared for her has travelled with me over the years. I wonder why Papa Ukwu's gods were able to remove a pregnancy but could not save her from AIDS.

*

My best friend and I are sitting in Kings Heath park when she breaks the news to me. She's HIV positive.

Shock. Disappointment. Sadness. They all move through me at once.

Funny, but it seems as if I am reflecting her emotions. All the questioning and self-criticism she must have been carrying since she found out.

How could my sensible, intelligent, fabulous friend be living with this virus? I could hardly bring myself to say the letters. H. I. V. This was an illness I associated with promiscuity, homosexuals and people living on the African continent. After all, these were the group of people in the 'high risk' categories. Like my cousins who had died twenty years before. So much had changed on the HIV/AIDS landscape, and yet so much hadn't changed.

I move closer, put an arm around her. The person I knew better than anyone. She leans into me and places her head on my shoulder and weeps and weeps and weeps. It's as if this understated action of mine has given her permission to let go.

Together we sit in the stillness of the afternoon. The sun struggles behind a cloud. Against the grey, her skin looks ashen. Around us, the trees seem bereft, as if even they have been touched by the magnitude of our sorrow.

This diagnosis could not have come at a worse time. Three months before her wedding to the man she had waited thirty-five years for. That's how she always phrased it. And I would joke, well you weren't waiting for a husband from birth. We would giggle at each other. But now, there was no laughter — only tears and heartbreak.

[20]

I remember the fitting we had for her. I sat on a comfortable avocado-green velvet sofa as she twirled in the wedding dress she'd decided on. An A-line gown with a plunging back. She sparkled: her dress, her shoes, her eyes. Although I had noticed that she'd been losing weight, and seemed worn, she swelled with joy. I'd asked her if she was okay and she'd brushed away my anxious expression with a smile. I assumed the demands of her teaching job and her wedding plans were taking its toll.

Many questions form and fall away.

How had she contracted this disease? Who had passed on the virus to her? Why had this happened? Funny that these were the thoughts that flitted in my mind at the time. As if the answer to any of these questions mattered. What difference did it make, the How, Who and Why? All that was important was that my beautiful soul-friend was suffering.

The next four weeks are a blur of hospital appointments and cups of tea. Her CD4 count stood at 118 — below the 200 line where if she fell ill with the flu or pneumonia, she could be said to have an AIDS-defining illness. From my research, I found that the virus, which attacks the immune system (CD4 cells), caused a weakening in her ability to fight off infections. If HIV is not treated, the gradual deterioration of the immune system leaves the body vulnerable to serious illnesses it would normally be able to fight off. She had to go on meds right away.

So, after more blood tests, conversations with the dietician and pharmacist, we went together to the local chemist at Heartlands and picked up three months' worth of antiretrovirals. A person living with HIV in the Global North, treated with antiretrovirals, will maintain an undetectable viral load, and establish a strengthened immune system. In the West, there has been a shift in the 1980s HIV/AIDS trajectory, from certain death to living with a manageable disease. However, the stigma still remains. As I help her place the package of medication into a Tesco Life Bag, I get a sense that this is still a disease that cannot be spoken of. The stigma of an HIV diagnosis means it is often a disease which is managed in private and in secret. This was a secret we now shared.

We make our way down the escalator to the café. For some reason, I'm ravenous and devour a chocolate croissant and latte. She has a pot of tea and a muffin, which she only picks at. She talks, as if in a stream of consciousness. How could she go through with the wedding? When she had informed her husband-to-be, he had promptly fucked her using three condoms. Hurt. Humiliated. Rejected. How had she become a statistic?

This was the question I would come back to many times over the next few months.

*

'The result has come back positive.' The doctor pauses, watches my facial expression. 'You're HIV positive...' He swipes at the wasp again. 'I know it wasn't what you wanted...'

I am falling in this dream.

Into shades of light: lavender, oyster and aubergine – sweet rich Jerusalem aubergines stewed in my mother's cooking.

Dark bruised mist.

Doctor Wescott's jaw narrows again – speaks words I do not want to understand. And I continue to fall into the slippery silence.

Patterns and shadows chase me, crowd me –

A tunnel of unravelling red.

Red.

Red.

Red.

The girl who fell into the Omoba well is there. Was her name Ugochi or Nneka? Mushrooms spring up all around; grey and beastly. They expand and rise and explode. Magenta ash circles my length – tightens; I splutter when it fills my lungs.

I will die.

[22]

Identity

Memories from my birthland, a place of soot and grime.
The Omoba yard where Mama Ukwu's kitchen

funnelled tales among wafts of goat pepper soup.
Plantain and yam, oxtail and tripe stew, prepared

in Mother's kitchen for special occasions.
On other days: plain pancakes sweetened

with lemon and sugar, peanut butter on thick-cut
bread from the local village store. A bowl

of porridge with Carnation milk swirled in . . .
Mama Ukwu talked and talked, dropped off;

head bopping, pulled-down lips dribbling,
snores deepened, lengthened 'til her morning Milo.

I am all these things: plantains, pancakes and pulled-down lips.

Omoba Village

Under an expansive ube tree,
Papa Ukwu sits on a bench.

Mama Ukwu roasts fresh cassava;
the *gari* blows all over the ground.

Dede Azubike climbs palm tree, whistles
at a girl with guava-shaped breasts

and cornrow hairstyle. Dressed
in indigo cloth, she carries

a bucket on her head,
a naked albino child on her back.

Motionless *onyinyo* form, dance
as if to the tune of *ndi ekpo*

and their lanterns. The swish-swish
of a besom fills the compound.

onyinyo – shadows
ndi ekpo – masquerades

Is that the doctor speaking or the rattlings of my thoughts? The aroma of *okazi* soup fills my nostrils as a buzz echoes.

Black and yellow markings appear on the far corner of the blinds.

A wasp.

Dull hues, hairs on legs twitch – then flight and buzz. Round and round and round. The doctor swipes at it, a heavy swat.

Misses.

It enters the walled tunnel of my mind, disappears into red confusion. Each word Doctor Wescott pronounces punches me in the stomach. I am losing my balance. A sudden hailstone downpour.

I need to hear what he is saying, but I focus on the battering against the window pane. I can't feel my legs in this non-place happening to me.

Buzz – Buzz – Buzz –

Everything in this office is cream or silver or red. Beside cream lamp stand: a silver shelving unit stacked with boxes of condoms. A dispenser of latex gloves. A leaflet on HIV/AIDS transmission. A bowl of red ribbons. The wasp circles the bulb. Petal-thin wings flit, zig-zag, before making a diagonal swoop, hovering for a moment in front of the doctor's face.

He stands, picks up a file.

Bursts of feathery blue reappear in my tunnel.

The drone of the wasp, now a drilling – deep and painful.

A hoist. A hot air balloon transporting all the men I slept with. A laugh – tumbling, waterfall laughter. He doesn't see me. None of them see me. Which one of them did this to me? The blue become grey ripples, rippling past my falling self.

Fallen.

Falling.

Fading – me or the tunnel.

[23]

Can Doctor Wescott hear me? I scream, beg my legs to find a way out of this tunnel. The words lodge in my throat. I see images. Red ribbon. Condoms. Hot air balloon.

I need to leave. Surely it can't be happening to me.

It is a dream.

*

In 2017, I travel to South Africa. In a township, I meet a tall gaunt man, sitting on the steps, leaning against the door of his half-painted cement house. Sipping water from an aluminium mug, his movements steady and painful, he speaks slowly, each word an effort. Antiretroviral medication is available, but he has no funds for transport to go to the clinic where the medicine is dispensed. He has no money to pay for the medication. And, more importantly he cannot afford food for himself, his son and grandson who is going blind. The gaunt man invites me to the local Pentecostal Church he attends. After a fifteen-minute walk, we arrive at a rectangular cement building at the end of a rocky path. At the entrance, he steadies himself on the stick supporting his frail body and leads me to a bench at the back of the hall. The space is packed with people on their feet, swaying and singing, with hands raised to the roof. The pastor, a bulky man, sweats profusely as he paces the wooden stage. As the singing ends, he bends over a Bible on the mahogany lectern. Fragrant candles waft the air. A baby's cry punctuates the pastor's flow, then there's silence. The pastor shouts: 'God has the power to heal all disease! Did he not raise Lazarus from the dead?' He carries on listing characters in the New Testament whom Jesus healed. When he is done, he calls those who are sick to the front, that they too may be healed. He continues to whip up the gathered: 'Faith is all you need. God is ready to heal you. The doctors have no power, only God has that authority. Even AIDS is nothing to God. Is medication stronger than God?' He punctuates these statements with a flurry of speaking in tongues. The faithful respond fervently, including my tall gaunt companion: 'Lord if you're willing, you can make me clean.'

[24]

These beliefs are just as strongly held by the African diaspora living in the U.K. I know of pastors in Black-majority churches who encourage them to stop treatment and focus on prayer. It is therefore no wonder such edicts promote a culture of non-disclosure, whereby if a person tells a pastor that they are HIV positive, a judgement on their faith may follow. Because if I am a true believer in God, and I am still suffering with this disease, is my faith not strong enough? It is frightening such messages are not being challenged more strongly, especially as many of these people living with HIV/AIDS are integrated in our communities up and down the country. If people are not empowered to speak honestly about their status, and driven to hide their diagnosis, then there will be more people living with HIV who are ignorant of their positive status.

My cousins Ugochi and Nneka died in a time when little was known about the illness. They visited traditional healers because they didn't have the money to go to medical doctors. Then and now, HIV/AIDS in African communities is understood as a curse, associated with immorality, promiscuity and recklessness. It is hard to see the difference between traditional healers and their incantations to the gods of my ancestors, and these charismatic preachers and their prayers to Almighty Jehovah. Both perpetuate the stigmatising profile of living with HIV/AIDS and drive people into leading secret, private and anonymous lives. As I write this, I wonder if my cousins would have fared any better in contemporary times, living in Nigeria where people still subsist in abject poverty, struggle to speak of HIV or AIDS, and would rather say a family member died of TB or malaria or an unknown illness — than name their shame.

*

My cousins find me in my dreams.

Often they are in my mother's kitchen. The aroma of bitter leaf soup and crayfish fills the room. My mother washes dishes at the sink, as my cousins and I eat a bowl of fruit: mango, papaya and pineapple

chunks. Onions and peppers sting my eyes. My mother returns to the stove, dips a ladle in the pot and tastes it. I try to speak to Ugochi and Nneka but before I can, they fade, and a chalice appears. Silver-plated with a floral motif around its middle. My eyes focus on a procession of lips – thin, thick, rouged, chapped. At the altar rail, heads dip forward, taste the alcohol, then jerk backward. I am behind Ugochi and Nneka in the queue. My heart quickens.

When it's my turn, I grasp the silver cup and bring it to my lips.

The wine turns to blood in my throat.

Water

mmiri

Relationship

A note to my mother

Red leaks from virginal labia,
keeps me on toilet seat,
frightened, unable to move.

What will I say to my mother?
How will I explain all this bother?
The bloody mess on tiled floor,
the stain on my new school skirt.

I sit and wait,
not sure what to do.

I use my pinky,
form a U,
feel sticky wet;
more red escapes.

Finger released,
whiff of rich iron and Bovril —

Eleven, and unsure
if I might be dying.
I try to stay calm,
with each deep breath.
Focus on smudged handprint
by the light switch.

But what will I tell my mother?

The Way It Was with You
A note to my father

Sour-faced and stern.
Left with you for a month
while Mum was away, we had

little to say from sunrise to sunset
You went to work and I — I stayed
home, wrestled with algebra

sums, or read a book by C.S. Lewis,
till it was time to cook a meal for two.
My soggy rice riled. 'Will you ever

be a good wife like your mother?'
I didn't blame you. The rice was salty,
not helped by the half-done mutton.

You grunted and spat; left half a plate
untouched, plus un-chewed fat. After
our evening meals, a heavier silence

clung to the curtains. You, nose-deep
in a newspaper with your legs extended
across the coffee table — I retreated

to my bedroom, opened the window,
listened to a distant thunderstorm
and watched rain fall.

Salford Canal

Pintail, with serenity of a bearded Buddha,
glides and weaves around limp condom.
She travels under a tunnel behind

red-and-yellow narrowboat,
steered by a sour-looking man
in mushroom-coloured coat.

Cyclist whizzes past graffiti-marked wall.
I tie sloppy shoelace: fall into jog,
press on with mid-morning solace.

Ella

Flautist from Wales – Cardiff or Llandudno,
I don't know which. With a tiny waist
and puckered expression; her chatter

rolls in ripples, with the enthusiasm
of a couple of JWs trying to sell God.
She stops, licks her lips, peers at me.

From the lens of my camera, I glimpse
her see-through greys, linger over
raised nipples against cotton vest.

She leans back on the wall; munching.
With a taffeta laugh, she offers a fork:
'Kath, come have some sushi.'

I release the shutter and accept the invite.

Textures

Eager for nutty Ethiopian brew,
sweetened by tingles from last night.

> *I embrace the fall of cool and smooth*
> *silk sheets crumple, tumble around*

Tidying fly-away braid beneath scarf,
I observe yolk gel plop into hot pan.

> *shoulders, breasts, hips and toes.*
> *Moonlight accentuates your curves.*

A slice of avocado and smoked salmon
placed on toasted bagel. Dash of salt.

> *I stroke your dark, damp mane*
> *(spread out like an Oriental fan)*

On the windowsill, a cock-sized cactus
and a bottle of migraine pills…

> *my mind, a tangle of sighs and whys.*

Eccles Stage

Hovels with gargoyles and cheeky charm.
Hoary curls bounce around tea mugs
in café brimming with 1940's tales.

In the library square, a group of leery louts
deface a bench with lighters and penknives.
One looks at me with pinched glabella.

I want to say something. Instead, I turn away,
stride towards the grim Post Office building.
We are all Beatles dolls playing our parts.

Adolescence

Caterpillars
wet, clear
wriggle southward
down
car window.

At the bus shelter,
a man with eczema
puffs a cigarette,
rubs his phallus.

Turbaned social worker
rushes by, on a bicycle,
to assess a teen,
who wets his bed
because dad's dead.

These fairytales
play out in my head,
as I bite
an unripe plum.

Celeste

Apricot rouge on permanent pout.

French-chic; dressed in replica haute couture,
as if she's just stepped off a Chanel catwalk.

She winks through severe designer frames,
and unzips knee-length pointy boots.

Balanced on one foot, then the other,
she slips boots off, saunters to the kitchenette.

Hollers with Mancunian twang, 'Tea, coffee?'
At my desk, I stifle a chuckle. A togged-up

faux pas of cultural conundrum,
she's no different from *moi, n'est-ce pas*?

Banana Spider

In Manchester zoo,
behind glass, glands
weave sticky threads,

golden-yellowish silk
reflects sunlight, attracts
stare of this brown bee,

trapped in another web,
destructive love affair,
with a man twice my age.

Change

Ball of string lodged in throat.
Took nine months
to breathe,
to cough,
not choke –
dislodge the knotted ball

Cull nine weeks of being with child.
Amelia. Noah. Freya.
Expanded breast sacs,
bloated abdominal tissue –
Sudden. Gone. Numb.

Hand rubs emptied cave,
remembers bloodied sea.
Pug-faced counsellor
tugs at the string of silent
emotions knotted –

Loosens
Pulls
Until
the words form and fall
unravelling grief.

Cube of Blue

In this blue room
metallic memories escape:
Yvonne's sudden death,
red-ribbon diagnosis,

marriage meltdown.
In cube of blue,
loss climbs on loss,

lizards scrabbling on lizards.
The sudden whiff of camphor –

A reminder of a time before cubed blue.

The Distance Between Us
A note to my husband

A strand has crept between us,
an unnoticed trespasser at our marital table.

Thread of discontent journeys
from your cortex to my tippy toes.

Zigzags from my knees to your elbows,
struggles to connect opposing trajectories.

To eat Vegemite or peanut butter?
To live in Birmingham or Bendigo?

We are nowhere, and the distance between us grows.

Gone

Berry, pea, seed
describe a non-being
coming or succumbing?

Stirrups and gel: a story ends
thought, emotion;
twisted pain, insane

tears fill dimmed room.
Indigo nails chipped;
indignant steel.

Sour lips press polystyrene,
sip ice-cold water.
Succumbed. Again.

Small Talk

fills the walls these days.

punctuated, forced;
hours spent keeping up

appearances, bone-tired
longings frayed over

many many months. burlap
cut-outs we've become

trammelled by life's bric-a-brac.
between spoonfuls of muesli

baby monitor goes off.
looking up, masks meet,

held in silence. I rise,
attend to the bundle

gurgling, in the only room
that makes sense.

Stacked and Stuffed

Five years of clutter boxed up.
Fifty-two cluttered boxes
stacked
stuffed
into storage.

Journals, photos, mementos,
squeezed in tattered cardboard
of brown and beige
stacked
stuffed

Boxed-up lovers, like patients
in psych wards.
Cramped images:
packed up
stacked up

until further notice.

Knotted

Right brain responds to pain.
Knotted tissue muscle
linked to a relationship in knots.
Chitchat revolves around
the sofa-bed in the study

Should it be folded or not?

Heated discussion over bills.
Tensions boil over. I take
cover, go to my hideaway.
You stay on the sofa, play
a game on iPhone.

If only men were from Mars
and women were from Venus,
perhaps this tide of conflicting egos
could be overlooked. Different
species, so does it really matter?

It does matter. It does matter.

If only marriage were simpler,
came with a handbook on how
to manage tiffs over *Whose turn
it is to buy the groceries?* or *Sweetie
will you take out the rubbish bins?*

Postpartum

Blood droplets on razor.
She sits cross-legged,
stares at a mirror, weeping
weeping, weeping . . .

She weeps
for lost joy
buried
under hours and hours
of baby feeds, changing nappies,
washing soiled beddings,
nursing colicky child.

Cherry-red globules
curdle in her nightmares.
Swollen breasts, leak.
A mother on the brink, in need
of a different kind of drink.
If only blood did not stain linen.

Golden Shovel
after John Burnside's 'Like Father'

Red lanterns dangle along washing line. I'm
drunk on cheap vodka and wine. Can hardly stand. I dance blind

with Maurice, bestie of twenty plus years. He allows me to
lean on sweat-soaked chest. I sway: sing, sing, sing. My

eyes, blood-shot, sting salty tears; worst
night of my life. Stumble, fall. Lifetime of mistakes

swell my belly until — until I purge and
purge and purge. I die that night, travel beyond

mushrooms and dead baby girl, on the road to redemption.

Fake News

Filth in every room
and I WANT OUT,
a trout on a river bank.

I ignore cobwebs,
dustballs, tufts of hair
clinging to kitchen tiles.

I knead dough for bread:
eggs, soya milk, buckwheat flour,
leave for an hour

listen to the news
lies lies lies
incessant, flit, confuse

the puddle of my mind
what does peloid mean?
left brain searches an answer

thoughts stuck, soiled
in mud mud mud
a thud interrupts, disrupts:

daughter of a witchdoctor's son
niece of a great mad aunt
Grandma had dementia at sixty-two.

Repentance

I ran out of time
in my checklist of life:
portfolio career, PhD, promotions,
marriage and mothering.

I had many adventures to distant lands:
Morocco, Malawi, and the Maldives.
Took photographs of a faux sadhu, vitiligo beggar
and children
with dreams of eating
pasta and pizza and polenta cakes.

I pushed twelve-hour days,
microwaved all meals,
peddled at the gym,
longing for Christ's 'abundant life'.

When I fell ill, the desire
to carry a child grew and kicked
inside me, but eggs
were in decline. I heard
the fading cry of children
lost before they became:
there were three.

Years spent salsa dancing,
drinking mango smoothies,
smoking hookahs, sexing it up,
and sailing dinghies.

I wanted it all — but
I wanted it all — but

Springtime

Sun loiters, unwanted
visitor on hill crest.

My skull's drum
spins thoughts,
chases the darkness.

Unending cycle,
chirruping blackbirds,
and four-wheel drive.

A brief interlude:
the sprawling ivy
ceases to frighten.

Black thoughts return.
Intolerable pincer pain.

Séance

I come alive through her breath,
the flesh that once was.

I, the marionette veiled behind
kohl smudged eyelids — I stir;

pulse through varicose veins,
girth enlarged with sugar cane.

She gives me voice: *Onye ekpo*
reaches into a worldly realm

talks to my husband and only child.

onye ekpo - masquerade

Dear X

A squatter's poison,
your touch has left me cursed,

the memory of your assault
with a co-joined twin; bedmate,

friend and pernicious foe.
My identity has changed;

flawless, no more – I
am stained, your handprints

tattooed on negroid skin.
We have become welded;

nickel wrought in furnace,
I cannot escape you

as you feed on me like a
tsetse. But who will die first?

The invincible you,
or the invisible I?